Genetics

CHRISTINE TAYLOR-BUTLER

Children's Press®
An Imprint of Scholastic Inc.

Content Consultant
Phyllis Meadows, PhD, MSN, RN
Associate Dean for Practice, Clinical Professor, Health Management and Policy
University of Michigan, Ann Arbor, Michigan

Library of Congress Cataloging-in-Publication Data
Names: Taylor-Butler, Christine, author.
Title: Genetics / Christine Taylor-Butler.
Other titles: True book.
Description: New York, NY : Children's Press, an imprint of Scholastic Inc.,
  [2017] | Series: A true book
Identifiers: LCCN 2015048717| ISBN 9780531218617 (library binding) | ISBN
  9780531227794 (pbk.)
Subjects: LCSH: Genetics—Juvenile literature. | Genetics—History—Juvenile
  literature.
Classification: LCC QH437.5 .T396 2017 | DDC 572.8—dc23
LC record available at http://lccn.loc.gov/2015048717

Front cover: Identical twins
Back cover: Illustration of DNA molecules

Find the Truth!

Everything you are about to read is true **except** for one of the sentences on this page.

Which one is **TRUE**?

T or F Humans have roughly 140,000 genes.

T or F Researchers discovered the structure of DNA with the help of photographs.

Find the answers in this book.

Contents

Chromosomes

THE **BIG** TRUTH!

Anatomy of DNA

3 Genetic "Fingerprints"

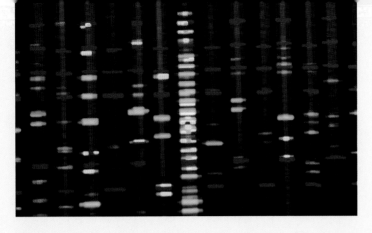
DNA sequence

Dolly, a cloned
sheep

Genes are the reason
every person is unique.

What Is Genetics?

Have you ever wondered why you look different from the people around you? Chemicals in your body called genes determine the blueprint for your appearance. Your genes were passed down to you from your mother and father. Their genes were passed down from their parents. Genes contain the building blocks necessary for all life on Earth. The study of genes and how they are inherited is called genetics.

 Genes are found in every cell in your body.

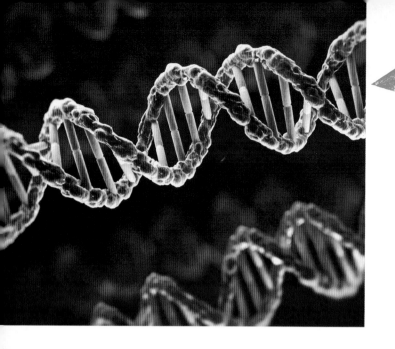

You can think of genes as a set of "instructions" that tell your body how to build itself.

Countless Combinations

Genes are contained in **molecules** called DNA. That is shorthand for deoxyribonucleic acid. DNA is not limited to just people. All living organisms contain it, including plants, animals, **bacteria**, and **viruses**. Genetics can explain why some people have brown eyes and others have green eyes. Or why some people come down with certain diseases and others do not. Genes determine everything from height to skin and hair color.

Because there are millions of combinations of genes, most people have a unique genetic code. Only identical twins share similar genetic codes.

Biologists who study DNA are called geneticists. But this is actually a fairly recent term. At first, most people didn't understand genes because they couldn't see them. Instead, scientists often guessed based on their observations of the world around them.

Identical twins can be very difficult for people to tell apart.

Darwin's Big Ideas

One scientist who studied how **traits** are passed on was Charles Darwin, an English biologist. Between 1831 and 1836, he traveled the world. During the trip, he collected **specimens** and kept notes. He believed that animals and plants that adapted to a particular environment were more likely to thrive and have offspring. Those that couldn't adapt would not survive. Darwin also thought that changes in the environment caused changes to a species as the organisms adapted.

Charles Darwin's theories helped lead to the modern study of genetics.

Darwin noticed, too, that plants that were self-**fertilized**—or whose offspring received all their genes from a single parent plant—were less healthy. Similarly, people who married close relatives had sicker kids.

In 1859, Darwin published a book of his theories called *On the Origin of Species*. The book was an instant best seller. At the time, scientists didn't know about DNA or genes.

Darwin's grandfather also studied evolution.

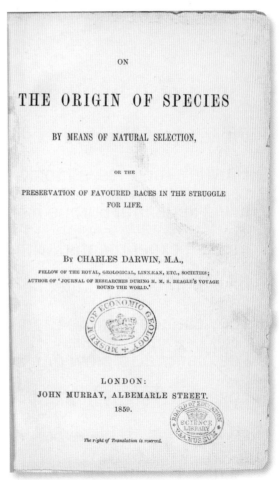

ON

THE ORIGIN OF SPECIES

BY MEANS OF NATURAL SELECTION,

OR THE

PRESERVATION OF FAVOURED RACES IN THE STRUGGLE
FOR LIFE.

By CHARLES DARWIN, M.A.,

FELLOW OF THE ROYAL, GEOLOGICAL, LINNÆAN, ETC., SOCIETIES;
AUTHOR OF 'JOURNAL OF RESEARCHES DURING H. M. S. BEAGLE'S VOYAGE
ROUND THE WORLD.'

LONDON:
JOHN MURRAY, ALBEMARLE STREET.
1859.

The right of Translation is reserved.

The Origin of Species (originally published as *On the Origin of Species*) is still widely read and discussed.

Mendel could grow two generations of pea plants each year.

Laws of Inheritance

While people studied Darwin's theories, a monk living in Central Europe had ideas of his own. Gregor Mendel experimented with pea plants. Pea plants have both male and female **reproductive** parts. They could **pollinate** themselves or another plant. Pea plants also grow quickly. This allowed him to observe changes in plant offspring over several generations. In his experiments, Mendel bred pea plants that produced yellow seeds with pea plants that produced green seeds.

Those plants' offspring produced only yellow seeds. But when the offspring self-pollinated, future generations produced green seeds 25 percent of the time. Mendel concluded that something passed from parents to offspring that determined what trait they would have. He also concluded that some traits are more **dominant** (such as yellow seeds), and others are **recessive** (such as green seeds). He published his findings in 1866. His conclusions are known as Mendel's Laws of Inheritance.

Though Mendel mainly studied pea plants, his findings apply to other species as well.

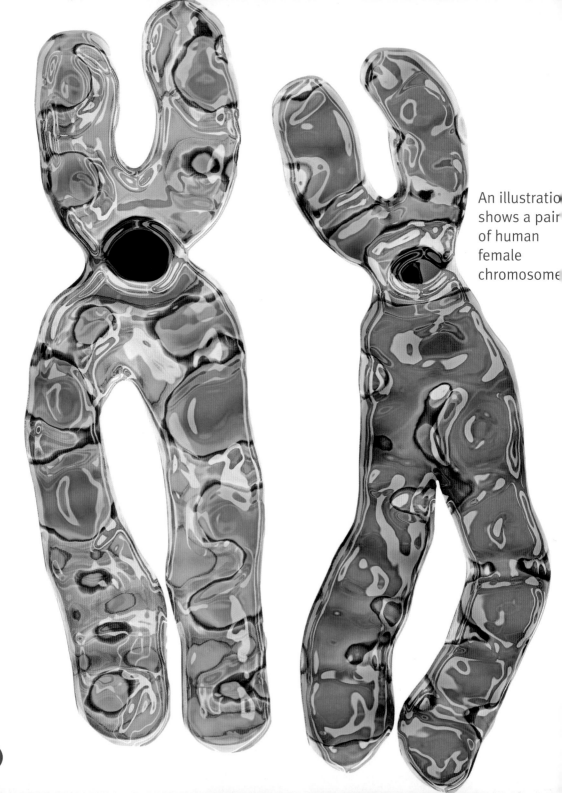

An illustration shows a pair of human female chromosomes

The Genetic Breakthrough

As early as 1842, scientists had discovered the existence of chromosomes. Chromosomes are "packets" of DNA found in every living cell. But no one understood exactly what roles chromosomes played. In 1905, Dr. Nettie Stevens discovered that a single chromosome pair determined an organism's sex. By breeding mealworms, she discovered that the male offspring contained a chromosome pair she labeled XY. Females had an XX pair.

Morgan's Fruit Flies

In 1908, Stevens's former professor, Thomas Hunt Morgan, began a study of the common fruit fly. Morgan knew from his work that most fruit flies have red eyes. One day, a white-eyed fruit fly flew into his laboratory. Morgan called the trait a **mutation**. In other words, the gene pattern that determined eye color was changed in the white-eyed fly. Morgan started breeding fruit flies with the mutation and tracking the traits each offspring displayed.

Fruit flies are still used in genetic research today.

Fruit flies breed quickly and have only four pairs of chromosomes to track. Morgan and his students grew the flies in milk bottles and created maps of each generation's mutations. The first generation of flies had red eyes like their parents. White eyes appeared in one out of four flies in future generations, similar to Mendel's plant experiment. But only male flies had the white eyes. Why?

Morgan's work was published in a book called *The Physical Basis of Heredity*.

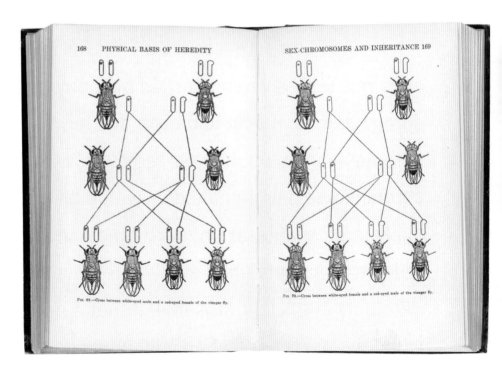

168   PHYSICAL BASIS OF HEREDITY

SEX-CHROMOSOMES AND INHERITANCE 169

Fig. 69.—Cross between white-eyed male and a red-eyed female of the vinegar fly.

Fig. 70.—Cross between white-eyed female and a red-eyed male of the vinegar fly.

Thomas Hunt Morgan exchanged letters with Nettie Stevens to learn more about her research on chromosomes.

Morgan concluded that the trait for white eyes was recessive and carried only on some X chromosomes. If a fly had even one red-eye X chromosome, it would have red eyes. With an XX chromosome pair, female flies would be more likely to have at least one X chromosome with the red-eye trait. Males had an XY chromosome pair. With only one X chromosome, if that X had the white-eye trait, the fly had white eyes.

The Alphabet of DNA

Scientists now had a better idea of how chromosomes worked. By 1950, researchers grew closer to solving another piece of the genetic puzzle. At Columbia University, Erwin Chargaff discovered something about four chemicals found in human DNA—guanine (G), cytosine (C), adenine (A), and thymine (T). The level of guanine always matched that of cytosine, and adenine was equal to thymine.

He discussed this with researchers James Watson and Francis Crick, but they weren't interested.

Chargaff's formula, G=C and A=T, is now known as Chargaff's Rules.

Photo 51

The invention of X-ray crystallography in Paris brought scientists even closer to understanding DNA. With X-ray crystallography, researchers could see the three-dimensional structure of a molecule. In 1951, Dr. Rosalind Franklin and assistant Raymond Gosling used this technique to photograph DNA. One image showed a **helix**, or three-dimensional spiral, structure with two strands. Franklin labeled it Photo 51.

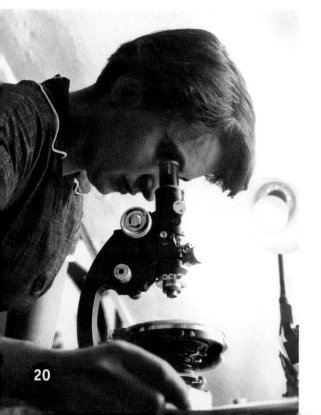

Rosalind Franklin's X-ray images were an important stepping-stone to understanding the structure of DNA.

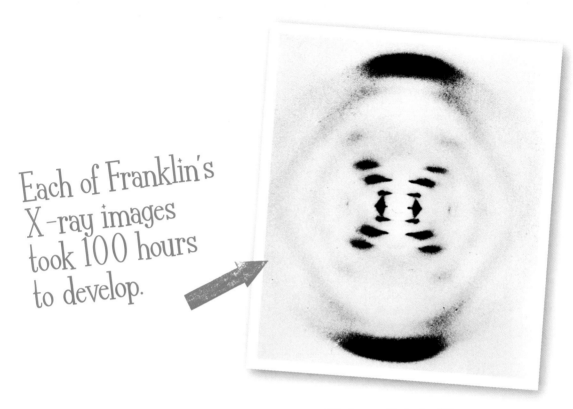

Each of Franklin's X-ray images took 100 hours to develop.

Fellow scientist Maurice Wilkins didn't like having a woman sharing his lab. He took Franklin's notes and photographs to his colleagues, Watson and Crick, without permission. Watson and Crick were trying to build a model of DNA. However, their design was based on incorrect assumptions. Seeing Franklin's Photo 51, they realized that it and Chargaff's formula were the keys to building a correct DNA model.

Watson (left) and Crick (right) show off their model of a DNA molecule.

Watson and Crick published an article on the structure of DNA molecules in 1953. In it, they described the shape as a double helix, just as Franklin's photo had shown. They gave Franklin no credit for her years of research or her role in the discovery. Franklin died of cancer on April 16, 1958. In 1962, Watson, Crick, and Wilkins received the Nobel Prize for their role in DNA's discovery.

Dolly the Sheep

In 1996, scientists in Edinburgh, Scotland, created a genetic copy of an adult sheep. This is called cloning. They first removed DNA from an unfertilized egg. They replaced it with the DNA taken from a cell from a donor sheep. The egg was then implanted in a third sheep, where it developed as any other lamb would until it was born. The lamb was named Dolly. Dolly lived for almost six years. This is about half the normal lifespan for a sheep.

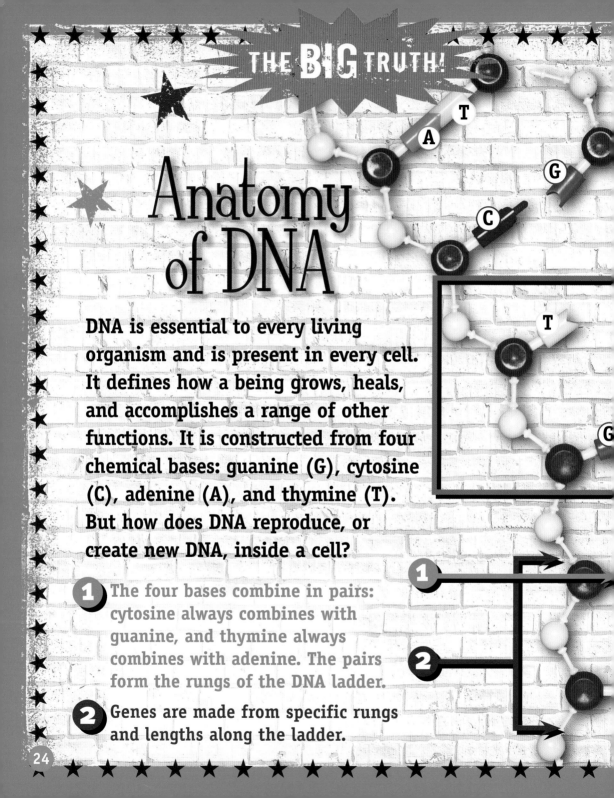

Anatomy of DNA

DNA is essential to every living organism and is present in every cell. It defines how a being grows, heals, and accomplishes a range of other functions. It is constructed from four chemical bases: guanine (G), cytosine (C), adenine (A), and thymine (T). But how does DNA reproduce, or create new DNA, inside a cell?

1 The four bases combine in pairs: cytosine always combines with guanine, and thymine always combines with adenine. The pairs form the rungs of the DNA ladder.

2 Genes are made from specific rungs and lengths along the ladder.

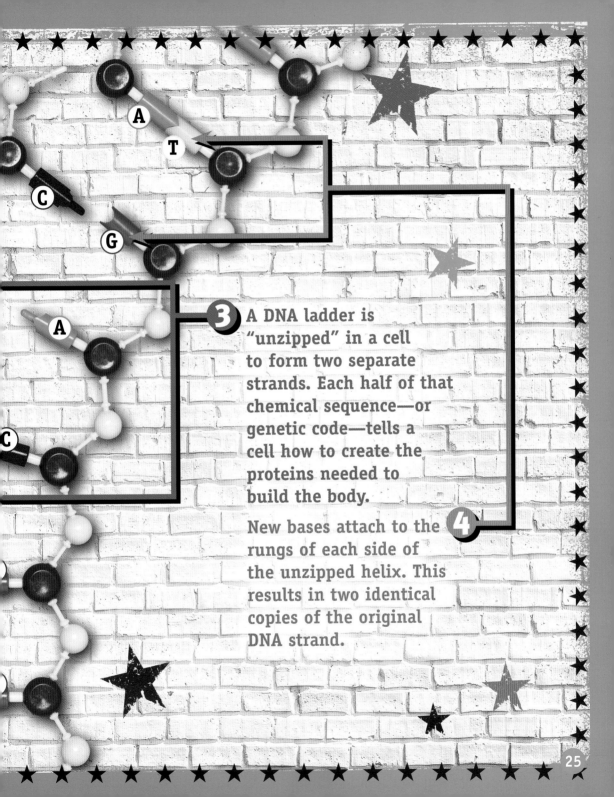

3 A DNA ladder is "unzipped" in a cell to form two separate strands. Each half of that chemical sequence—or genetic code—tells a cell how to create the proteins needed to build the body.

4 New bases attach to the rungs of each side of the unzipped helix. This results in two identical copies of the original DNA strand.

It takes about eight hours for a human cell to copy its DNA.

Because of shared chromosomes, children usually look a little bit like each of their parents.

CHAPTER 3

Genetic "Fingerprints"

Once scientists cracked the DNA code, they used the information to advance modern scientific knowledge. Every person has 46 chromosomes: half from his or her mother, and half from his or her father. Each person's chromosomes are completely unique. With this in mind, Sir Alec Jeffreys suggested in 1978 that a single test could identify people based on those genetic markers. He proved in 1984 that the technique worked. It is known as DNA fingerprinting.

A scientist collects DNA evidence from a crime scene.

A Biological Encyclopedia

DNA fingerprints contain a wealth of information. Sir Jeffreys was able to use them to identify and reunite kidnapped children with their biological families. DNA fingerprinting also helped the British government confirm the ancestry of foreigners wanting to live there. Now, law enforcement around the world uses the test. It helps them identify suspects in criminal investigations and free innocent people.

Could a DNA fingerprint also help solve medical mysteries? Dr. Mary-Claire King thought so. Her research led to the discovery of an important gene mutation known as BRCA1. BRCA1 is responsible for inherited breast and ovarian cancer. People with the mutation have a higher chance of developing the disease than those without it. Testing for the mutation is now used to identify cancer risk in patients with family histories of the disease.

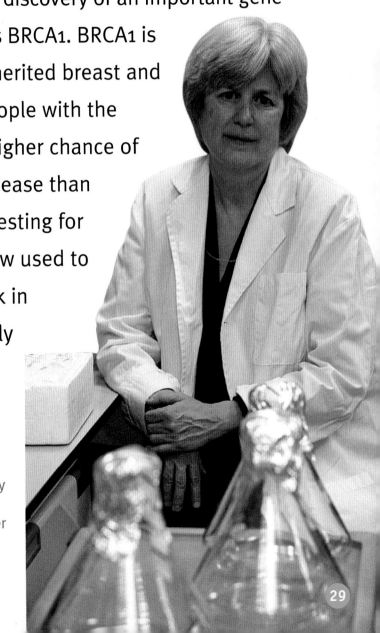

Dr. Mary-Claire King's discovery has helped many people avoid the medical issues caused when cancer is left undiscovered.

After King's discovery, laboratories rushed to clone the BRCA1 gene to use in testing. One company, Myriad, filed a patent, meaning only Myriad could control the gene. The company charged $3,000 each time someone used its test to screen women for breast cancer. It even demanded King stop using the gene she discovered. In June 2013, the U.S. Supreme Court put a stop to the greed. The justices ruled that genetic material in its natural form could not be patented.

A simple blood test can be used to determine whether a patient is at risk of breast and ovarian cancer.

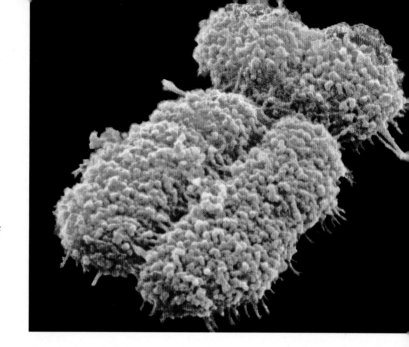

Telomeres, shown here in orange, are located at the tips of chromosomes.

Genes and Aging

DNA research continued. Dr. Elizabeth Blackburn discovered an enzyme, a type of protein, that plays a role in aging. This enzyme, called telomerase, creates a protective "cap" called a telomere. It covers the ends of chromosomes and determines how often a cell divides. As people age, the telomeres grow shorter. This causes cells to age as well. Dr. Blackburn noticed that stress and trauma also shorten the telomeres and cause premature aging.

A person's DNA sequence can look like this.

Genetics in Modern Use

The Human Genome Project is an international program created in 1990 to map every gene in the human body. Scientists once thought there were between 50,000 and 100,000 genes. However, by 2003, 100 percent of the estimated 3 billion base pairs were mapped. The project found only about 20,000 human genes exist. It also discovered that other living organisms have similar genes performing similar functions.

The Human Genome Project cost $2.7 billion to complete.

Medicine

Genetic mapping helps identify traits that cause disease. Newer studies may actually cure them. A growing health risk is diabetes. Diabetes occurs when the body cannot produce insulin, a substance needed to reduce blood sugar. Currently, many people with diabetes take insulin shots each day to treat the disease. But scientists are testing gene therapy to eliminate the need for insulin shots. Tests show a single gene therapy shot may control insulin for six weeks.

Timeline of Genetic Understanding

1866
Gregor Mendel publishes an article on his Laws of Inheritance.

1859
Charles Darwin publishes *On the Origin of Species*, which defines how species change over time.

THE ORIGIN OF SPECIES

BY MEANS OF NATURAL SELECTION,

PRESERVATION OF FAVOURED RACES IN THE STRUGGLE FOR LIFE.

By CHARLES DARWIN, M.A.,

LONDON,
JOHN MURRAY, ALBEMARLE STREET,

1905
Nettie Stevens discovers that a single chromosome pair—XX or XY—determines an organism's sex.

Genetic Discrimination

Sometimes laws struggle to keep up with scientific discoveries. For example, mandatory genetic testing invades a person's privacy regarding his or her health. It can also lead to discrimination against people with genetic diseases. In 2001, the U.S. government sued Burlington Northern Santa Fe Railroad for secretly testing employees for genetic diseases. In 2008, a new law officially banned the practice, protecting all workers from genetic discrimination.

1953
A series of discoveries lead to the first accurate model of a DNA molecule.

1996
A lamb named Dolly is born, becoming the first successful clone of an adult sheep.

2003
Researchers with the Human Genome Project complete the mapping of every gene in the human body.

Researchers in Thailand cloned a swamp buffalo for the first time in 2011.

The FDA received more than 30,000 complaints about its 2008 cloning decision.

Cloning the Food Supply

With the success of cloning Dolly the sheep, researchers began cloning more livestock. In 2001, the U.S. Food and Drug Administration (FDA) requested a temporary halt to selling cloned animals for human consumption. They wanted to test the products to ensure their safety. They found some of the clones had birth defects. However, the FDA concluded in 2008 that meat and milk from cow, pig, and goat clones were safe.

Genetically Modified Organisms (GMOs)

Another controversial use of genetic engineering is to modify the genes of food crops. Genetic material that is not naturally occurring is inserted into seeds. Some seeds are altered to resist disease, pests, or weed killers. Others are modified to better survive drought. Some scientists suggest these crops are safe. Others say more research is needed to be sure.

Foods labeled "organic" are not genetically modified.

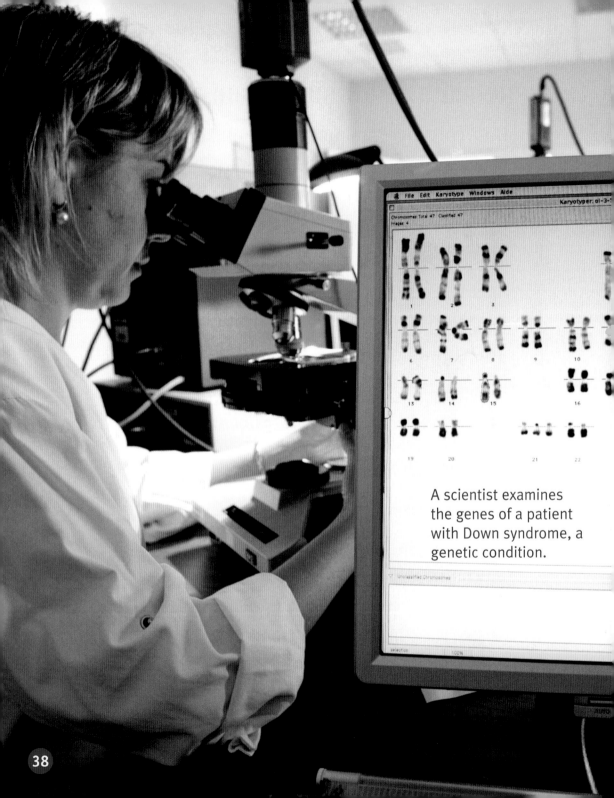

A scientist examines the genes of a patient with Down syndrome, a genetic condition.

CHAPTER 5

The Future of Genetic Research

Genetic research allows patients and doctors to identify who is likely to become sick from some diseases. Some people may have an organ removed if a family history shows it may develop incurable cancer. Others screen to make sure a disease isn't passed to their children. But genetic research has also raised many ethical questions. If genetics can be used for good, can it also be harmful?

Humans have 46 chromosomes. Dogs have 78. Cats have 38.

Human Cloning?

When doctors transplant a heart, liver, or kidney, they worry the patient's body will reject it. Scientists believe it may be possible to create a new organ that is an exact DNA match. They would do this by using the genetic material from a person's own cells. But should science go further? What if it were possible to clone an entire person?

A nurse carries a transplant heart to surgery in a protected cooling container.

VITALPACK

GREFFE D'ORGANE
URGENT

ce conteneur doit voyager

Predicting the Future

Out of roughly 2,000 genetic diseases, only a few dozen are serious or start when a person is an adult. Genetic testing has become more affordable over time, making it accessible to more people. Some people have used it to learn more about their ancestry. However, some experts argue that people shouldn't screen for genetic mutations. It might cause them to change their lives, worrying about something that may never happen.

One day, all you might need is a DNA sample from the inside of your cheek to create a full map of your genes.

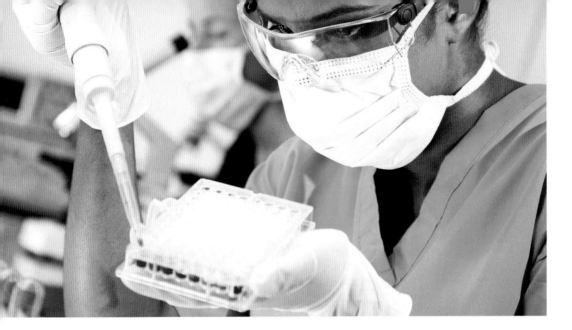

There are many possible careers for people who are interested in the field of genetics.

What Would You Do?

Since ancient times, people have experimented with plants and animals. They have sought to create stronger species. Would creating a new species be good for the planet or bad? What if you accidentally introduced a new disease? If you could decide what things to do with genetics, what would you choose? These debates will likely continue for years to come. Will you be one of the people helping decide? ★

Immortal Genes

In 1951, Henrietta Lacks was receiving treatment in a hospital. A doctor took samples of her cells without permission. Scientists discovered that her cells, now called HeLa cells, never died. Since then, HeLa cells have been used to create cures and vaccines all over the world. They've been studied in space. They have also been discovered everywhere. Even in the air. Many medical discoveries could not have happened without Henrietta Lacks's immortal genes.

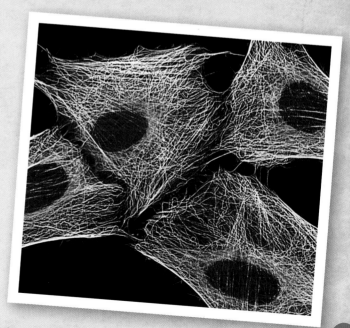

True Statistics

Number of chromosomes in a human: 46

Number of chromosomes in a mouse: 40

Number of chromosomes in some bacteria, such as *E. coli*: 1

Number of chromosomes in a dog: 78

Percent of DNA that every human shares, on average: 99.9

Percent of DNA shared among humans, chimpanzees, and bonobo apes: 98.8

Combined length of the DNA from all the cells in your body: About 6,000 million mi. (9,700 million km)

Percent of a human's DNA that consists of genes: About 1

Percent of a human's DNA whose function is not yet understood: About 97

Did you find the truth?

 F Humans have roughly 140,000 genes.

 T Researchers discovered the structure of DNA with the help of photographs.

Resources

Books

Mooney, Carla. *Genetics: Breaking the Code of Your DNA*. White River Junction, VT: Nomad Press, 2014.

O'Neal, Claire. *Projects in Genetics*. Hockessin, DE: Mitchell Lane Publishers, 2011.

Visit this Scholastic Web site for more information on genetics:
★ www.factsfornow.scholastic.com
Enter the keyword **Genetics**

Important Words

bacteria (bak-TEER-ee-uh) microscopic, single-celled living things that exist everywhere and can either be useful or harmful

dominant (DAH-muh-nint) most influential or powerful

fertilized (FUR-tuh-lizd) to begin reproduction in an animal or a plant

helix (HEE-liks) a spiral shape

molecules (MAH-luh-kyoolz) the smallest units of a substance that still have all the characteristics of that substance

mutation (myoo-TAY-shuhn) a change in a gene

pollinate (PAH-luh-nate) to carry or transfer pollen from the stamen to the pistil of a flower or flowers so that female cells can be fertilized to produce seeds

recessive (ree-SES-ihv) less dominant or powerful

reproductive (ree-pruh-DUHK-tiv) having to do with the production of offspring

specimens (SPES-uh-muhnz) samples or examples used to stand for a whole group

traits (TRAYTS) qualities or characteristics that make one person or thing different from another

viruses (VYE-ruhs-iz) very tiny organisms that can reproduce and grow only when inside living cells

Index

Page numbers in **bold** indicate illustrations.

About the Author

Christine Taylor-Butler is the award winning author of more than 75 books for children including a middle grade science fiction series: The Lost Tribes. Her True Book on Rosa Parks was named to the American Library Association's 2015 Amelia Bloomer list. A graduate of the Massachusetts Institute of Technology, Christine holds degrees in both Civil Engineering and Art and Design. She lives in Kansas City, Missouri.